Culinary Austria

The best and most famous dishes

We would like to thank:

Rosenthal Österreich
Kärntner Straße 16
1010 Wien
Tel. 01 / 512 39 94
Fax: 01 / 512 14 66
E-Mail: office@rosenthal.at

First published by 2006 by Hubert Krenn Publishing, Vienna, Austria - www.hubertkrenn.at

Culinary Austria
The best and most famous dishes

Recipes by Helmut Deutsch
Translation by Hubert W. Krenn
Photography by Fotostudio Riedmann, Robert Marksteiner, Peter Torker
Design by Peter Furian and Georg M. Thellmann - www.furian.at
DTP by Mama Resl
Printed in Austria by Druckerei Theiss GmbH, A-9431 St. Stefan

ISBN 3-902532-02-5

Culinary Austria

The best and most famous dishes

KRENN

Contents

Each recipe serves four unless an alternative number is given. Measurements are given in both metric and imperial. Use either in any one recipe, as they may not always be exact conversions. Cooking times are a guide. They can vary according to the ingredients, or the individual equipment.

Abbreviations:
kg......................kilogram
g..............................gram
l.......................................liter
ml ....milliliter
lb...........................pound
oz........................ounces
pt .... pints
tbsp.............tablespoon
tsp .... teaspoon

Glossary

Beuschel: stew with innards
Brösel: breadcrumbs
Buchteln: baked yeast buns
Fisolen: green beans
Frittaten: sliced pancakes
Grammeln: pork cracklings, pork rinds
Gugelhupf: the cake takes its name from the form in which it is baked
Knödel: dumplings
Krapfen: doughnuts
Kraut: cabbage
Kren: horseraddish
Marille: apricot
Nockerln: small dumplings
Powidl: plum sauce
Sachertorte: the famous Austrian pastry
Semmel: bread roll
Spätzle: a batter-like dough, pressed into small dumplings
Strudel: paper thin pastry, filled with fruits
Topfen: curd
Wiener Schnitzel: veal cutlets, coated in bread crumbs
Zwetschke: plums

Conversions formulas
for american, british and metric measures:
ounces to grams -
X the ounces - 28,35
grams to ounces -
X the grams - 0,035
liquid ounces to milliliters -
X the ounces - 29,57
milliliters to liquid ounces -
X the milliliters - 0,03
inches to centimeters -
X the inches - 2,54
centimeter to inches -
X the centimeters - 0,39
Fahrenheit to Celsius -
X the fahrenheit - 5/9 (after subtracting 32)
Celsius to Fahrenheit -
X the celsius - 9/5 (then add 32)
X = multiply

British dry measures for ounces and pounds are the same as American measures. The British liquid ounce is 1.04 the American ounce.

Pork Crackling Spread

Grammelaufstrich

Ingredients:

200g (7 oz) pork cracklings
3 eggs, boiled and chopped
2 mixed pickles, sliced
50g (1 ¾ oz) onions,
finely chopped
2tbsp of clarified butter
2 cloves of minced garlic
salt, pepper

Mince the pork cracklings and fold in eggs, pickles, onions and butter.

Season to taste with garlic, salt and pepper and serve with bread.

Potato Spread

Kartoffelkäse

Ingredients:

400g (14 oz) potatoes,
boiled and peeled
250ml (8fl oz) sour cream
80g (2 ¾ oz) cream
100g (3 ½ oz) chopped onions
caraway
chopped fresh parsley
salt, pepper

Peel the boiled potatoes while warm and strain them through a ricer or a food mill. Mix with fine cut onions and the other ingredients.

To serve spread the cheese on brown bread and garnish with parsley.

Liptauer Spread

Ingredients:

300g (10 ½ oz) butter
300g (10 ½ oz) soft cheese,
made from sheep milk
150g (5 ½ oz) onions minced
70g (2 ½ oz) capers
2 sweet sour pickles
2tbsp finely chopped parsley
salt, pepper
grounded caraway
garlic, paprika powder
anchovy paste

Beat the butter creamy and add the strained cheese. Mix it gently while adding the finely minced onions, pickles, capers and parsley. Season to taste with salt, pepper, caraway, garlic, paprika powder and anchovy paste.

Serve with bread.

Photo: Pork Crackling Spread

Herring Salad with Beetroots

Heringssalat mit Roten Rüben

Ingredients:

200g (7 oz) celery, cut in sticks

120g (4 oz) pickled herring, cut in larger pieces

250g (9 oz) potatoes, boiled, peeled and cubed

150g (5 ½ oz) mixed pickles

250g (9 oz) apples, cut in sticks

salt, pepper

sugar, mustard

125ml (4fl oz) sour cream

100g (3 ½ oz) mayonnaise

2 boiled beetroots

100g (3 ½ oz) onions, diced

First cook the celery sticks in saltwater. Then cut the pickled herrings in larger pieces. Thinly cut the boiled and peeled potatoes, pickles and apples in cubes.

Mix it all together in a bowl, add mayonnaise and sour cream and season with salt, pepper, mustard and a hint of sugar. Fold in the beetroots and onions. Adjust the seasoning, to taste.

This dish tastes best when covered and refrigerated for a few hours.

Serve as a salad.

Beef Stock
Rindsuppe

Ingredients:

1 kg (2lb 4oz) beef marrow bones

500g (1lb 2 oz) beef

200g (7 oz) root vegetables (carrots, parsnips, celery)

1 large leek, parsley sprigs, celery leaves

1 onion, unpeeled

salt

1tsp peppercorns

1/2 bay leave

1 garlic clove

freshly grated nutmeg

Place the cut beef bones in boiling water and bring it to a short, hard boil, strain the water and just quickly rinse the bones with cold water. Transfer the bones into a large stockpot or saucepan, add cold water and bring to the boil. Add the meat and bring to the boil again. Skim off any foam that rises to the surface.

Halve the onions, fry in a pan without fat until brown and add to the broth. Add the washed and chopped vegetables, the garlic and the herbs. Reduce the heat to medium low and simmer, uncovered, for 3 hours.

Remove the meat and strain the stock, bring it to a boil once again and skim off any foam or fat. Season to taste with salt and nutmeg and garnish with chives.

Small Semolina Dumplings
Grießnockerln

Ingredients:

50g (1 ¾ oz) butter

1 egg

100g (3 ½ oz) fine semolina

salt

freshly grated nutmeg

Beat the butter creamy and whisk the egg with a fork, gradually stir into the butter. Stir in the semolina and season it with salt and nutmeg. Cover and leave to rest for 15 minutes. Use two spoons to form small dumplings and lay them on a oiled platter. Put in the refrigerator to chill for 15 minutes.

Cook the dumplings in boiling salted water, reduce the heat and simmer, partially covered, for 20 minutes.

Photo: Beef Stock with Semolina Dumplings, Sliced Pancakes (p. 12) and Liver Dumplings (p. 13)

Savoury Sponge Diamonds
Biskuitschöberl

Ingredients:

3 egg yolks
3tbsp cream
3 egg whites
50g (1 ¾ oz) plain flour
salt
butter and flour for the baking tray

Beat the egg yolk with salt. Whisk the egg whites until it forms soft peaks. Fold the whites to the yolk mixture, and whisk in cream and flour. Spread the mixture to the thickness of a finger on a buttered and floured baking tray. Bake in the preheated oven at 200° for 10 minutes. Leave to cool, than cut into diamonds or squares. Add to the soup just before serving.

Imperial Sponge Diamonds
Kaiserschöberl

Ingredients:

60g (2 oz) butter
3 egg yolks
2tbsp milk
3 egg whites
2tbsp cheese, grated
80g (2 ¾ oz) plain flour
salt
freshly grated nutmeg
butter and flour for the baking tray

Beat the butter until light and fluffy, add egg yolk and milk, season with salt and a pinch of nutmeg. In a separate bowl, whisk the egg white until it forms soft peaks. Fold the white, flour and cheese gently through the yolk mixture. Spread the mixture to the thickness of a finger on a buttered and floured baking tray. Bake In the preheated oven at 200° for 10 minutes. Let it cool, than cut into diamonds or squares. Add to the soup just before serving.

Sliced Pancakes
Frittaten

Ingredients:

250ml (8 fl oz) milk
120g (4 oz) plain flour
1 egg
2tbsp fresh parsley, finely chopped
salt
freshly grated nutmeg
oil for frying

Combine milk and flour carefully. Fold In the eggs and finely chopped parsley and season with salt and nutmeg. Whisk until the batter is smooth. Cover and leave to rest at room temperature for 15 minutes. Heat the oil in a suitable pan, scoop 1/4 cup of the batter into the skillet, and cook for about 30 seconds, until small bubbles form on the top of the pancakes. Turn it over and cook for about 30 seconds longer or until golden brown. Cool the pancakes then cut into thin slices. Add to soup just before serving and sprinkle with parsley.

Liver Dumplings
Leberknödel

Soak the bread in cold water and squeeze dry. Fry the onions until golden brown. Mix liver, onions and bread, and add the remaining ingredients and knead for a minute.

Leave to rest in a cool place for 15 minutes. Form small balls and cook them in slightly boiling salted water for about 15 minutes.

Add to the soup.

Ingredients:

150g (5 ½ oz) beef liver, trimmed and finely chopped

1 bread roll

2tbsp onions, finely chopped

oil for frying

70g (2 ½ oz) bread crumbs

1 egg

salt

pepper

marjoram

1 garlic clove

parsley, finely chopped

Bread with Milt Cream
Milzschnitten

In a frying pan heat butter and fry onions and milt. Stir in eggs and the seasonings until totally combined. Leave for rest to cool down.

Spread the mixture on one side of the bread slices. Heat 1 cm oil in a pan, fry the bread with the coated side bottom down first and then turn around. Fry until golden brown. Drain on kitchen paper and cut in stripes or cubes.

As an alternative the bread could also be baked in the oven.

Add to the soup.

Ingredients:

80g (2 ¾ oz) milt from beef, scraped from the skin

30g (1oz) onions, finely chopped

1tbsp butter

2 eggs

4 slices white bread

parsley

salt, pepper

marjoram

1 garlic clove

Viennese Potato Soup
Wiener Kartoffelsuppe

Ingredients:

50g (1 ¾ oz) bacon

50g (1 ¾ oz) onions, sliced

20g (¾ oz) butter

20g (¾ oz) plain flour

1l (2 pints) beef stock

100g (3 ½ oz) root vegetables (carrots, parsnips, celery)

20g (¾ oz) dried wild mushrooms

100g (3 ½ oz) potatoes, peeled and cubed

salt, pepper, marjoram

Heat the butter in a large stock pan, fry the sliced onions with bacon, add some flour and stir occasionally. Add beef stock, as well as vegetables, mushrooms and season with salt, pepper and marjoram. Let it simmer for 10 minutes.

Add the potatoes to the broth and continue to boil until the potatoes are tender.

Season to taste with salt and pepper.

Goulash Soup
Gulaschsuppe

Ingredients:

200g (7 oz) onions

4tbsp oil

20g (¾ oz) paprika powder

20g (¾ oz) tomato paste

200g (7 oz) beef

200g (7oz) potatoes, cut in cubes

salt

pepper

garlic cloves, finely chopped

caraway seeds

marjoram

Fry beef and onions in a large pot until golden brown. Add paprika-powder, tomato paste and pour in some water. Toss to mix. Add the beef stock and season with salt, pepper, garlic, ground caraway and marjoram. Reduce heat, cover the pan and simmer for 30 minutes.

Add then the peeled and cubed potatoes to the broth and continue to boil until tender.

To serve check the seasoning.

Styrian Pumpkin Soup
Kürbiscremesuppe

Ingredients:

500g (1 lb 2 oz) squash (pumpkin)
80g (2 ¾ oz) onions, finelly chopped
40g (1 ½ oz) butter
2 garlic cloves
½tsp Paprika powder
1 bay leave
1l (2 pints) beef stock
salt
pepper
caraway
¼l (8fl oz) cream
80g (2 ¾ oz) pumpkin seeds
20g (¾ oz) butter
125ml (4fl oz) cream, whipped
1tbsp pumpkin seed oil

Halve the squash lengthwise and scoop out the seeds. Cut in smaller pieces. Place it in a larger stockpan and pour in the stock. Season with herbs and simmer until the squash is very soft. Remove the bay leave and blend the soup, add the cream and check for seasoning. Simmer over a low heat.

Garnish with pumpkin seeds, whipped cream and pumpkin seed oil.

Stew with Innards
Beuschel

Ingredients:

1/2 lung of veal

1/2 heart of veal

300g (10 ½ oz) root vegetables (carrots, parsnips, celery)

50g (1 ¾ oz) onions, finely chopped

60ml (2fl oz) white wine

60g (2 oz) oil

60g (2 oz) plain flour

salt, peppercorns, thyme, bayleave, marjoram

a dash of vinegar

mustard

For the Special-Seasoning:

2 mixed pickles, 1tbsp capers, 1 anchovy fillet, 2tbsp onions, finely chopped, 1 garlic clove, lemon zest, parsley

Rinse heart and lung in cold water. Pour water in a large pot, add lung and heart, root vegetables, onions and season with salt, peppercorns, thyme and bayleave. Bring it to a hard boil, reduce heat and simmer, covered, until the lung is tender. Remove the lung from the pot and place it in slightly saltet, cold water and leave to cool down. Leave the heart in the pot until tender, then cut heart and lung in stripes and marinate with white wine. Pour the liquid through a strainer in a bowl and set aside.

Heat oil and sprinkle with flour, add the Special-Seasoning, stir until golden brown. Pour in a dash of vinegar and the strained stock, season with mustard, lemon juice, marjoram and salt. Cook until sauce thickens, then add the innards, bring it to the boil and season to taste.

Stew with Innards and Goulash
Salon Beuschel

Ingredients:

Stew (see above)

125ml (4fl oz) sour cream

125ml (4fl oz) goulash gravy

Prepare the stew as seen above. Just before serving mix in sour cream and goulash.

Bread Dumplings
Semmelknödel

Ingredients:

3 bread rolls or good stale bread – at least a day old

50g (1 ¾ oz) butter

30g (1 oz) onions, chopped

60ml (2fl oz) milk

1 egg

salt, parsley

20g (¾ oz) plain flour

Cut the bread in cubes and roast it in a frying pan with butter. Roast the onions, add parsley and put aside to cool down. Combine milk and egg, season with salt, and pour the liquid and the roasted onions onto the bread cubes. Sprinkle with flour, give it a short rest, and form with your hands bigger dumplings, like the size of a tennis ball. Cook gently, uncovered, in boiling water.

Fried Potatoes with Black Pudding

Blutwurstgröstl

Ingredients:

600g (1lb 5oz) black pudding

50g (1 ¾ oz) bacon

500g (1lb 2 oz) potatoes, cooked and peeled

100g (3 ½ oz) onions, finely chopped

2 garlic cloves

marjoram

2tbsp clarified butter

salt, pepper

Cut black pudding, bacon and the cooked potatoes in pieces. Mince onions and garlic.

Heat concentrated butter in a large frying pan, stir in black pudding slices, onions and ham.

Add the peeled and cubed potatoes, season to taste with marjoram, salt and pepper and roast well.

Serve with sourkraut or salad.

Potato Goulash
Kartoffelgulasch

Ingredients:

200g (7 oz) onions
50g (1 ¾ oz) bacon
60g (2 oz) oil
60g (2 oz) paprika powder
1 tsp vinegar
800g (1lb 12 oz) potatoes,
peeled and cubed
250g (9 oz) sausage
water
salt

Goulash-Spices:

1 tsp marjoram
1 tsp caraway seeds
2 garlic cloves, finely
chopped

Finely mince the onions and fry in large heavy pot with oil and paprika powder. Add a hint of vinegar, pour in some water and season with gulash spices. Peel and cube the potatoes and add to the pan and simmer, partially covered, until the potatoes are tender.

Cut the sausage in larger pieces, add to the goulasch and bring it to a short boil.

Meat Dumplings
Fleischknödel

Ingredients:

Potato dough (see below)

For the filling:

350g (12 oz) pork hash
50g (1 ¾ oz) onions, finely chopped
30g (1 oz) oil
salt, pepper
paprika powder
marjoram, parsley

Cook and hash the meat, mix with finely chopped onions and fry in oil. Season with salt, pepper, parika powder, marjoram and fresh parsley.

Roll out the dough as thinly as possible and cut in squares. Pleace the meatballs in the middle of a square and draw the dough up over to form a sealed dumpling. Drop the dumplings into hot water and cook gently.

Serve with warm sourkraut.

Dumplings with Pork Cracklings
Grammelknödel

Ingredients:

For the dough:

400g (14 oz) potatoes
caraway seeds, salt
freshly grounded nutmeg
60g (2 oz) plain flour
60g (2 oz) fine semolina
30g (1 oz) butter
4 egg yolks

For the filling:

100g (3 ½ oz) pork cracklings
50g (1 ¾ oz) onions, finely chopped
garlic, salt, pepper
1 egg

Peel the boiled potatoes and press through a strainer. Mix with semolina, flour, egg yolks, butter and salt and make a dough. Mince the pork cracklings and fry with onions. Season with salt, pepper and garlic. Mix with the egg and leave to cool down.

Roll out the dough out as thinly as possible and cut in squares. Pleace the porkcrackling balls in the middle of a square and draw the dough up over to form a sealed dumpling. Drop the dumplings into hot water and cook gently for 10 minutes.

Photo: Meat Dumplings

Tyrolean Dumplings
Tiroler Knödel

Ingredients:

300g (10 ½ oz) bread rolls
or good stale bread – at
least a day old

1 onion, finely chopped

200g (7 oz) butter

150g (5 ½ oz) ham, cut in
cubes

250ml (8fl oz) milk

2 eggs

3tbsp plain flour

fresh parsley, finely
chopped

salt

pepper

Put the cubed bread in a large bowl and add the roasted onions. Whisk the eggs and milk, and add the liquid with the melted butter, the finely chopped ham, parsley and flour to the bowl. Stir well and season with salt and pepper.

Put it aside and let it rest for 15 minutes. Form with your hands bigger dumplings, like the size of a tennis ball, and cook gently in boiling water.

Best served with salads or with beef stock. As a main dish serve with sourkraut.

Stuffed Peppers
Gefüllte Paprika

Ingredients:

500g (1lb 2 oz) mixed meat hash

50g (1 ¾ oz) rice, boiled and drained

4 bell peppers, green or red

1/2l (16fl oz) tomato sauce

Mix the meat hash with the cooked rice, season with salt and pepper. Around the stalk of each pepper, pull it off, taking the core with it. Spoon the stuffing into the peppers.

Stand them upright in an oiled baking tin and bake in the oven.

Meanwhile finish the tomato sauce, pour over the peppers and bake until the peppers are very tender.

Serve with boiled potatoes (p. 50).

Viennese Tomato Sauce
Wiener Tomatensauce

Ingredients:

500g (1lb 2oz) fresh, overripe tomatoes, chopped

500ml (16fl oz) beef stock

75g (2 ½ oz) ham or bacon

50g (1 ¾ oz) onions, finely chopped

30g (1 oz)root vegetables (carrots, parsnips, celery) chopped

20g (¾ oz) butter

30g (1 oz) plain flour

50g (1 ¾ oz) tomato puree

bay leave, salt

10g (2tsp) caster sugar

3 peppercorns

dash of vinegar

Place the tomatoes in a saucepan and cook with beef stock until tender. Combine butter, ham, onions and root vegetables in a separate sauce pan. Sprinkle with flour and sweat until the onions are soft. Add the tomato puree and the cooked tomatoes.

Season to taste with salt, pepper, sugar and the bay leave. Stir until totally combined, then press the liquid through a sieve. Check the seasoning. The sauce should be smooth and rich.

Carinthian Stuffed Pasta
Kärntner Kasnudeln

Ingredients:

For the dough:

160g (5 ½ oz) plain flour
20g (¾ oz) fine semolina
2 eggs
a dash of vinegar
1 egg yolk

For the filling:

250g (9 oz) Cottage cheese
100g (3 ½ oz) potatoes, cooked and mashed
125ml (4fl oz) sour cream
fresh mint
chervil
fresh chives & fresh parsley, finelly chopped
salt
1tbsp butter

First make your pasta dough. Work in flour, semolina, eggs and vinegar into a firm dough. Wrap in foil, and leave to rest.

For the pasta filling mix the potatoes with sour cream, melted butter, finely cut fresh herbs and Cottage cheese. Form small balls and set aside.

Roll out the dough. Using a knife or a wheel, cut out circles of 8 cm, brush with egg yolk and place the filling in the middle of the circle. Cover with the remaining dough, press them together and seal, twist slightly.

Cook the pasta in a large pan of boiling water, transfer them out of the pot with a slotted spoon, drain and rinse shortly with cold water.

Serve with melted butter and garnish with chives.

Cheese Spätzle

Käsespätzle

Ingredients:

500g (1lb 2 oz) strong plain flour
3 eggs
1/2l (16fl oz) milk
salt
pepper
freshly grated nutmeg
130g (4 ½ oz) cheese, medium
120g (4 oz) cheese, strong
50g (1 ¾ oz) clarified butter
50g (1 ¾ oz) onions, sliced

Sift the flour into a large bowl. Form a well in the centre and add the eggs, a pinch of salt and nutmeg. Beat the mixture lightly, it should be a very wet, soft dough. Bring a large pan of salted water to the boil. Set the spätzle press on top. Put the dough into the press or a colander and begin pressing it through the holes.

Cook in batches. As soon as the water rises, boil for about 30 seconds. Remove cooked spätzle out of the water with a slotted spoon, drain in cold water and place layers in a large roasting pan. Sprinkle each layer with grated cheese, salt and pepper.

Fill the pan with the spätzle and bake in the oven uncovered, until the cheese top layer is melted.

Slice onion rings and fry in gratified butter until golden brown.

When serving pour the butter over the spätzle and garnish with the onions.

Serve with salad.

Cabbage Pasta

Krautfleckerln

Ingredients:

500g (1lb 2 oz) cabbage white

100g (3 ½ oz) onions, finely chopped

100g (3 ½ oz) concentrated butter

30g (1 oz) sugar

salt

pepper

300g (10 ½ oz) pasta bows, farfalle or any kind of preferred noodles

Slice the cabbage and sprinkle with salt. Fry the finely chopped onions in butter, sprinkle with sugar and add the cabbage to the pan. Pour in water, season with pepper and cook until tender.

Meanwhile cook your pasta in boiling salted water according to packet instructions. Drain and mix with the cabbage. Season to taste.

Serve with salad.

Baked Ham Noodles

Schinkenfleckerln

Ingredients:

100g (3 ½ oz) onions, finely chopped

100g (3 ½ oz) butter

250g (9 oz) ham, diced

250g (9 oz) noodles or pasta

100g (3 ½ oz) butter

4 egg yolks

4 egg whites

40g (1 ½ oz) cheese, Emmentaler or medium strong cheese

250ml (8fl oz) sour cream

salt, pepper, marjoram

finely chopped parsley

butter and breadcrumbs for the frying pan

Fry the onions and ham in a suitable pan. Meanwhile cook your pasta in boiling salted water according to packet instructions. Drain and mix with the ham and season to taste with salt, pepper and marjoram.

Beat the butter creamy and stir in the egg yolk. In a separate bowl whisk the egg whites stiff and thick. Carefully fold in cheese, sour cream and the whites in the yolk mixture. Stir to combine and add the pasta.

Take a ovenproof dish, brush with butter and sprinkle with bread crumbs. Pour the pasta mix in and spread evenly. Bake for 30 minutes with 180°.

Garnish with parsley and serve with salad.

Baked Trout Fillets

Gebratenes Forellenfilet „Müllerin"

Ingredients:

4 trout fillets about 150g (5 ½ oz) each, skinned

40g (1 ½ oz) plain flour

100g (3 ½ oz) butter for frying

1 bunch parsley, finely chopped

80g (2 ¾ oz) butter

lemon juice

salt

Brush the trout fillets well with lemon juice, season with salt, and dip the fish in flour on both sides to coat evenly. Heat a frying pan to medium high and fry on both sides until a light crust has formed. For the sauce add some butter, parsley and lemon juice and pour it over the fish.

Serve with boiled potatoes (p. 50).

Baked Trout Fillets with Almonds

Forellenfillet mit Mandeln

Ingredients:

4 trout fillets about 150g (5 ½ oz) each, skinned

40g (1 ½ oz) plain flour

100g (3 ½ oz) butter for frying

80g (2 ¾ oz) butter

100g (3 ½ oz) almonds, sliced and roasted

lemon juice

Worcestershiresauce

salt

pepper

Brush the trout fillet with lemon juice, Worcestershire-sauce, salt and pepper. Dip them in flour on both sides to coat evenly. Heat a frying pan to medium high and cook until it has a light crust. For the sauce add some butter and almonds to the pan and roast it. Before serving pour the sauce over the fish and garnish with parsley

Serve with fried potatoes (p. 48).

For grilling a whole trout use the same recipe.

Poached Trout

Forelle blau

Ingredients:

4 whole trouts, clean and deboned
1l (2 pints) water
3tbsp vinegar
20g (¾ oz) salt
50g (1 ¾ oz) parsnips
50g (1 ¾ oz) celery
80g (2 ¾ oz) onions, sliced
5 black peppercorns
1 bay leave

To prepare the court bouillon, combine the water, vinegar, onions, bay leaves and black peppercorns, in a sauce pan and bring to the boil. Reduce the heat, cover partially, and simmer for 20 minutes.

Place the fish in a fish kettle or another pan in which they will fit comfortable. Pour the bouillon into the pan to cover the fish. Simmer gently 10 to 12 minutes, partially covered, until the fish flakes easily when tested with a fork at the thickest point. Do not let the liquid boil dry.

Carefully lift the fish out of the bouillon and serve straight away with lemon halves and boiled potatoes.

Fried Carp Fillets

Gebackener Karpfen

Ingredients:

600g (1lb 5 oz) carp fillets
100g (3 ½ oz) flour
2 eggs
100g (3 ½ oz) bread crumbs
oil
lemon wedges
salt
lemon juice

Generously marinate the carp fillets on both sides with salt and lemon juice.

Coat the carp fillets in the flour, dip in the egg mixture and coat with breadcrumbs on both sides. Put the prepared fish into a frying pan and fry until brown on both sides. Carefully take out the fish, drain briefly on kitchen paper.

Serve with lemon halves and potato salad.

Photo: Fried Carp Fillets

Fried Chicken
Backhuhn

Ingredients:

1 chicken – quartered or jointed in 8 pieces

salt

plainflour

4 eggs

bread crumbs

oil for frying

1tbsp fresh parsley, chopped

lemon wedges

Remove any excess fat from the chicken pieces and trim off the wing tips. Rinse the pieces and pat thoroughly dry. Coat the chicken pieces in the flour, dip them in the egg mixture and coat in breadcrumbs.

Fry the chicken pieces, starting with the skin side up, until golden brown and cooked through carefully take out the pieces, drain on kitchenpaper. Chicken giblets (liver, stomach) can be fried as well.

Serve hot with lemon wedges, fried potatoes and salad. Garnish with fried parsley-leaves.

Potato Salad
Kartoffelsalat

Ingredients:

500g (1lb 2oz) potatoes

2tbsp vinegar

1/4l (8fl oz) beef stock

4tbsp oil

salt, pepper

sugar

60g (2 oz) red onions, finely diced

fresh chives, finely chopped

Put the potatoes in a saucepan and cover with cold water. Add salt and cook until tender. Drain and then cut them into 1/2 inch slices while warm.

Combine the vinegar, beef stock, oil, salt, pepper, a taste of sugar and the minced onions in a bowl. Blend well and fold into the potatoes.

Serve while warm and garnish with chives.

Stuffed Roast Chicken
Gefülltes Brathuhn

For the stuffing: Beat the butter and the egg yolks together. Season it with salt and nutmeg and mix it with the finely chopped parsley. Soak the bread rolls in milk, press them dry and sieve it. Add to the butter and gently stir in the thick and creamy egg whites and adjust the seasoning.

Rinse the chicken well, inside and out, under cold water. Pat it dry. Remove any excess fat from the bird, including the fat pockets around the tail. Season the chicken with salt and rosemary and fill with the prepared stuffing. Sew close with a large needle and heavy thread. And tie the legs together with kitchen string. Place the chicken on a large roasting pan and place the pan in the preheated oven at a temperature of 180° and roast until tender, basting occasionally with the pan juices. Transfer the bird to a carving board and let it rest.

Skim off the fat from the roasting juices and heat the de-fatted juices in a small saucepan along with any juices that have gathered on the carving board or chicken broth and pour it through a gravy separator. Remove the string, carve the chicken and serve with potatoes and sauce.

Cucumber Salad
Gurkensalat

Season the cucumber with salt and garlic, leave to rest. To make the dressing combine sour cream with pepper, sugar and water, flavoured with vinegar. Add the dressing to the cucumber and check the seasoning.

Veal Fricassee
Eingemachtes Kalbfleisch

Ingredients:

600g (1lb 5 oz) veal, cut in cubes
200g (7 oz) root vegetables (carrots, parsnips, celery)
40g (1 ½ oz) onions, diced
1 bay leaf
5 black peppercorns, salt
40g (1 ½ oz) plain flour
40g (1 ½ oz) butter
100g (3 ½ oz) peas, precooked
150g (5 ½ oz) cauli
150g (5 ½ oz) white mushrooms
30g (1 oz) butter
freshly grounded nutmeg
lemon juice
125ml (4fl oz) double cream
2 egg yolks

Heat butter and fry the veal with root vegetables, onions, bayleave, peppercorns and salt until tender.

In a smaller pan whisk the flour in melted butter and add some water, stir until totally combined. Pass the liquid through a strainer add the meat, vegetables, beas and cauli. Slice the white mushrooms, roast them in butter slightly and add to the meat. Adjust your seasoning with nutmeg and lemon juice.

Whisk the cream and the egg yolk and pour to the meat. Bring it to a short boil and serve with rice or Nockerln (p. 46).

Rice – Viennese Style
Reis „Wiener Art"

Ingredients:

1 tbsp butter
200g (7 oz) rice, water, salt
1/2 onion, spiked with cloves
3 cloves
1 tbsp butter

Heat the butter in a large saucepan, put in the rice and cook, stir with a wooden spoon to coat the grains well with the fat, for 2 minutes. Add the boiling water, season with salt. Spick the onion with cloves and put it in the rice. Reduce the heat to medium-low and simmer covered until the rice is tender and the liquid has been absorbed, for about 20 minutes.

Before serving, remove the onion, sprinkle with butter flakes and fork it in. Season to taste with salt.

Veal Goulash
Kalbsgulasch

Ingredients:

600g (1lb 5 oz) veal shoulder, cut into 1 ½ inch pieces
300g (10 ½ oz) onions
50g (1 ¾ oz) butter
20g (¾ oz) paprika powder
1 garlic clove
zest of ½ lemon in wide strips
lemon juice, salt
1tbsp tomato paste
125ml (4fl oz) sour cream
1tbsp flour
125ml (4fl oz) cream

Fry in large heavy pot the finely chopped onions and paprika powder. Add a hint of water, garlic, lemon zest, lemon juice and season with salt. Stir well and bring it to a hard boil. Add the veal, the tomato paste and the water. Reduce the heat und simmer gently, partially covered at a medium heat until the meat is tender. Take out the meat and pour the gravy through a gravy separator or a strainer.

Mix the sour cream with flour, stir into the gravy, add sweet cream and bring it to a short boil. Season to taste. Add the meat to the gravy and serve with sour cream topping as a garnish.

Small Buttered Dumplings
Butternockerln

Ingredients:

300g (10 ½ oz) plain flour, sifted
2 eggs
60g (2 oz) butter
salt
250ml (8fl oz) milk

Sift flour into a large bowl. Add a pinch of salt, eggs and melted butter. Stir in the milk and beat the mixture lightly. The consistence of the dough should be very smooth. Put the through a spätzle press or colander and begin pushing it through the holes. Or you can scrape it with a knife directly from the cutting board into the boiling water.

As soon as the water resumes boiling, give it a short boil. With a slotted spoon, transfer the dumplings to a cold waterbath, then drain well. In a frying pan melt butter, add the dumplings and toss well. Adjust with salt to taste.

Wiener Schnitzel

Ingredients:

600g (1lb 5 oz) veal
cutlets, trimmed

salt

plain flour

4 eggs

bread crumbs

oil to fry

lemon wedges

Cut the veal in 4 escalopes. Pound until thin and even in thickness. Make a few incisions round the edges. Salt the cutlets on both sides.

Coat the cutlets on both sides in flour, dip in egg mixture and coat in breadcrumbs. Bake the cutlets in hot oil on both sides until brown. Drain on kitchenpaper and serve with lemon halves.

Traditionally served with fried potatoes, boiled rice (p. 44), potato salad (p. 40) or cucumber salad (p. 42).

Fried Potatoes
Petersilkartoffeln

Ingredients:

900g (2lb) potatoes,
peeled and quartered

100g (3 ½ oz) butter

fresh parsley, finelly
chopped

salt

Peel the uncooked potatoes and quarter them. Cook in salted water for about 20 minutes, drain and fry in a pan with butter and fresh chopped parsley.

Pork with Horseraddish
Krenfleisch

Ingredients:

600g (1lb 5 oz) pork (shoulder)

bouquet garni (1 bayleave, 3 peppercorns) in a small muslin bag

100g (3 ½ oz) onions, finely chopped

300g (10 ½ oz) root vegetables (carrots, parsnips, celery), diced

1tsp vinegar

fresh parsley, finely chopped

fresh horseradish, grated

salt

Put the meat in boiling, salted water. Add the bouquet garni and bring it to the boil. Skim of any rising foam. Reduce heat and after 45 minutes, add the onions and the root vegetables. Cook until the meat is tender.

Lift the meat out of the pot, cut it in slices. Add to the remaining cooking liquid a scent of vinegar and season to taste.

Serve the meat sprinkled with fresh parsley, shredded horseradish. Garnish with the cooked root vegetables and pour some cooking liquid on top.

Best served with boiled potatoes.

Boiled Potatoes
Salzkartoffeln

Ingredients:

900g (2lb) potatoes, peeled and cubed

100g (3 ½ oz) butter

salt

Peel the potatoes and cut in cubes. Cook until tender, remove from the pot and toss in melted butter. Adjust to taste with salt.

Malt Beer Stew
Salzburger Bierfleisch

Ingredients:

600g (1lb 5oz) sirloin of beef

salt, pepper

80g (2 ¾ oz) gratified butter

100g (3 ½ oz) onion, chopped

150g (5 ½ oz) bacon

1 tbsp tomato paste

2 tbsp plain flour

250ml (8fl oz) dark malt beer

750ml (23fl oz) beef stock

marjoram, thyme

1 slice rye bread

2 slices of bacon

4 tbsp pickling onions

Cut the beef into large chunks. Heat the butter in a large heavy saucepan and add the beef. Fry until brown on all sides. Remove the beef from the pot.

Add onions, bacon, tomato paste, sprinkle with flour and stir. Heat it up and pour in the malt beer and the beef stock. Season with marjoram, thyme, salt and pepper. Add beef and cook, partially covered, until meat is tender.

As garnish fry the cubed brown bread with onions and bacon, season with salt and pepper and mix with the beef stew.

Best served with white bread dumplings or potatoes.

Crown Roast of Pork
Schweinsbraten

Ingredients:

1kg (2lb 4 oz) crown roast of pork, bones frenched

salt

garlic

caraway seeds

1tbsp flour

1/2l (16fl oz) beef stock

Preheat the oven to 350°. Brush the meat lighty with salt, garlic and caraway. Place the roast in a shallow roasting pan. Cover the tops of the bones with small pieces of aluminium foil to keep them from burning. Roast, basting occasionally with the pan juices. The crackling should be crisp and the meat tender and juicy. Since pork is bred so lean these days, it might be tender sooner.

Transfer the meat to a carving board, cover loosely with foil and leave to rest for 15 minutes. Meanwhile add to the pan juices beef stock, bring it to a hard boil, sprinkle with flour and stir until the sauce thickens. Season to taste.

Best served with rice, potato dumplings, potatoes, cabbage or salad.

Potato Dumplings
Kartoffelknödel

Ingredients:

500g (1lb 2 oz) potatoes, peeled

50g (1 ¾ oz) fine semolina

150g (5 ½ oz) plain flour

2 egg yolks

30g (1 oz) butter

salt

Peel the boiled potatoes and press through a strainer. Mix with semolina, flour, egg yolks, butter and salt and make a dough. Leave to rest for a while, then form with your hands dumplings and cook it in boiling, salted water.

This potato based dough can also be used for other fruit or meat dumplings.

Rostbraten a la Esterhazy

Esterhazy-Rostbraten

Ingredients:

600g (1lb 5 oz) rib or short loin of beef, sliced and trimmed

salt, pepper

2tbsp oil

500ml (16fl oz) beef stock

200g (7 oz) roots vegetables (carrots, parsnips, celery)

50g (1 ¾ oz) onions, finely chopped

30g (1 oz) butter

125ml (4fl oz) sour cream

1tsp flour

mustard

1tsp capers, finely chopped

lemon zest

fresh parsley, finelly chopped

Cut the meat in slices. Pound until thin and even in thickness and cut small slits into the edges of the meat. Rub it with salt and pepper, brown it in oil on both sides, pour beef stock and simmer for 30 minutes.

Cut the roots vegetables and the onions, roast in butter and add to the meat. Cook until tender. Whisk the sour cream with flour, mustard and stir in the gravy until thickened.

When serving garnish the dish with finelly chopped capers, lemon zeste and parsley. Best served with rice (p. 44), pasta or bread dumplings (p. 18).

Rostbraten a la Girardi

Girardi-Rostbraten

Ingredients:

600g (1lb 5oz) rib or short loin of beef, salt, pepper

2tbsp oil

100g (3 ½ oz) onions

125ml (4fl oz) white wine

500ml (16fl oz) beef stock

60g (2 oz) ham

70g (2 ½ oz) white mushrooms

50g (1 ¾ oz) onions

lemon zest

capers, finely chopped

fresh parsley, finely chopped

30g (1 oz) butter

60g (2 oz) plain flour

125ml (4fl oz) sour cream

65ml (2fl oz) sour cream

Cut the meat in slices. Pound until thin and even in thickness and cut small slits into the edges of the meat. Rub it with salt and pepper. Brown it in oil on both sides and transfer the meat off the pan. Roast the pan juices with onions, add white wine and pour in the beef stock. Put in the meat and cook the meat until almost tender.

Finely chop the ham, white mushrooms, onions, lemon zest, capers and parsley, roast it in butter and drizzle with some flour. Whisk in sour cream and put the meat to the gravy. Cook the meat for a few minutes until tender.

Season to taste and serve with sour cream topping. Best served with dumplings (p. 58).

Beef Goulash
Rindsgulasch

Ingredients:
600g (1lb 5 oz) beef
500g (1lb 2 oz) onions
100g (3 ½ oz) oil
1tbsp paprika powder
1tbsp tomato paste
a dash of vinegar
1tbsp Goulasch spice-mix (garlic, marjoram and caraway seeds)
salt
plain flour

Heat the oil, and fry onions and paprika powder in a large heavy pot. Stir well, and add a hint of vinegar, tomato paste, salt and the beef. Toss the meat with the spice mixture to coat it well.

Add the water and simmer gently, partially covered, for 2–3 hours until the meat is tender. To thicken the gravy, sprinkle flour on top and stir in gently.

Serve with boiled potatoes or white bread dumplings.

Beef Goulash Viennese Style
Fiakergulasch

Ingredients:
1 egg
1 sausage
1 sweet sour pickles

Add to the beef goulash fried eggs, a sausage and sweet-sour pickles. Garnish all ingredients on the goulash and serve with boiled potatoes.

Dumplings in a Napkin
Serviettenknödel

Ingredients:
5 bread rolls, cut into cubes – at least 1 day old
375ml (13fl oz) milk
6 eggs, salt
freshly grounded nutmeg
60g (2 oz) butter
butter
bread crumbs

Chop the bread rolls in small cubes. Combine milk, eggs, salt, nutmeg and melted butter and pour over the bread. Gently mix to form a dough and giving it the shape of cylinder. Set aside in room temperature. Wrap the dough in cling film and cook it in a large bowl for about 35 minutes. Using a sharp knife, cut the cylinder in slices. Garnish with in butter roasted bread crumbs.

Photo: Beef Goulash Viennese Style

Stuffed Beef Roulades
Rindsrouladen

Ingredients:
40g (1 ½ oz) bacon
40g (1 ½ oz) sweet sour pickles
40g (1 ½ oz) carrots
30g (1 oz) onions
4 beef cutlets
salt
pepper
mustard
40g (1 ½ oz) oil
1tbsp tomato paste
1/2l (16fl oz) beef stock
1/16l (2fl oz) sour cream
1tbsp plain flour

Chop the cucumber and carrot in sticks, dice the onions and cut the ham in cubes. Pound the escalopes flat and evenly in thickness, and season with salt, pepper and mustard. Spread the vegetables and the ham on the meat. Fold it over and roll the meat up. Roll tightly and tie string the meat or fix with toothpicks.

Place the roulade in a frying pan and cook quickly over medium heat, turning until well couloured. Transfer the roulade to a roasting pan. Heat the remaining oil with tomato paste, add the stock and simmer for 1 hour until the beef is tender.

Transfer the meat from the pan. Put the pan on the hob over medium heat and add cream and flour, bring it back to boil, then reduce heat and cook, until the sauce has reduced and thickened. When serving, remove the string, pour over the sauce and serve with buttered dumplings, mashed potatoes and vegetables.

Mashed Potatoes
Kartoffelpüree

Ingredients:
600g (1lb 5 oz) potatoes, peeled and cubed
80g (2 ¾ oz) butter
salt
freshly grounded nutmeg
250ml (8fl oz) milk
oil for frying
onions, thinly sliced

Peel and cut potatoes in larger cubes and cook in slightly salted boiling water. Remove from the pot and pass through a potato ricer onto a large bowl. Add butter, stirring gently with an eggbeater, season with salt and nutmeg and slowly pour in the milk just enough to make a good consistence of the mash.

For serving garnish with caramelised or fried onions.

Boiled Beef
Gekochter Tafelspitz

Ingredients:

500g (1lb 2oz) beef bones
50g (1 ¾ oz) milt
50g (1 ¾ oz) liver
1 bay leave
5 peppercorns
750g (1lb 11oz) beef, cut of upper rump
200g (7 oz) root vegetables (carrots, parsnips, celery)
50g (1 ¾ oz) onions, in their skin
salt
fresh chives, finely chopped

Put the bones in boiling water and bring to a hard boil. Remove from the pot and rinse with cold water. Pour cold water in a large saucepan, add bones, milt and liver, bring it to a boil and skim off any foam that rises. Add the meat, the herbs and 1 hour before the end of cooking time, the root vegetables and the onions.

After approx. 3–4 hours (total cooking time) remove the meat from the stock and strain the stock through a fine sieve.

For serving slice the meat, garnish with salt and chives and pour on some beef stock.

Horseraddish with Apples
Apfelkren

Ingredients:

500g (1lb 2oz) apples, peeled and cut in cubes
1tbsp lemon juice
1/4l (8fl oz) water, salt
1tbsp sugar
1tbsp freshly grated horseraddish

Peel the apples and cook them in seasoned with lemon juice boiling water. Pass the apples through a ricer or a food mill onto a small bowl, leave to cool down and add the shredded horseraddish to taste.

Chive Sauce
Schnittlauchsauce

Ingredients:

150g (5 ½ oz) white bread, crusts removed and cubed
1/2l (16fl oz) milk
2 egg yolks
3 eggs, hard boiled
1/2l oil, vinegar, mustard
white pepper, salt
3tbsp chives, finely chopped

Soak the bread in milk, press the liquid out and pass through a ricer or food mill onto a small bowl. Combine cooked egg yolk, egg yolk, salt, pepper and vinegar and mix, preferably in a blender, and stir in the bread.

Slowly pour the oil in a thin stream into the mixture and whisking until the sauce is thick. Stir in the cooked and finely chopped egg whites and chives.

Photo: Boiled Beef with Beans with Dill (p. 67), Potato Fritter (p. 66), Horseraddish with Apples and Chive Sauce

Rostbraten with Fried Onions
Zwiebelrostbraten

Ingredients:

600g (1lb 5 oz) rib or short loin of beef
salt
pepper
50g (1 ¾ oz) plain flour
2tbsp oil
1tbsp butter
40g (1 ½ oz) plain flour
1/2l (16fl oz) beef stock
500g (1lb 2oz) onions, sliced
50g (1 ¾ oz) plain flour
oil

Cut the meat in slices, pound until thin and even in thickness. Cut small slits into the edges of the meat. Rub it with salt and pepper. Coat one side with flour and brown it in oil on both sides, beginning with the floured side. Transfer from the pan and keep warm while cooking the juices, and frying the onions.

Put the pan on the hob over medium heat and add the flaked butter, scrape up the juices and give it hard boil. Then add the beef stock and stir until the mixture thickens. Season to taste.

Cut onions in rings or stripes, coat with flour and fry in hot oil.

When serving, pour the gravy over the meat and then cover with fried onions.

Fried Potatoes
Bratkartoffeln

Ingredients:

600g (1lb 5oz) small potatoes
oil, butter
salt

Cook the potatoes in slightly salted boiling water. Remove from the water, and peel and fry them in a pan. Remove the oil, add some butter and toss well. Season to taste with salt.

Potato Fritter
Geröstete Kartoffeln – Rösti

Ingredients:

500g (1lb 2 oz) potatoes, boiled
50g (1 ¾ oz) oil
100g (3 ½ oz) finely chopped onions
salt

Cook the potatoes in slightly salted boiling water, remove from the water. Peel and grate or thinly slice them. Fry the potatoes on medium heat until golden brown on both sides.

Season with salt.

Baked Potatoes with Bread Crumbs
Gestürzte Kartoffeln

Ingredients:

30g (1 oz) butter
30g (1 oz) bread crumbs

Butter a baking tin and sprinkle with bread crumbs. Add the potatoes and bake in the oven for 30 minutes until the top is golden brown. To serve pour the potatoes at once on the serving platter.

Glaced Sauted Carrots
Glacierte Karotten

Ingredients:

800g (1lb 12oz) small baby carrots or peeled, sliced carrots
60g (2 oz) butter
1tsp sugar, salt
beef stock
fresh parsley, finely chopped

Put the carrots in a hot sauté pan with butter and sugar. Add some beef stock, turn and toss the carrots until tender.

To garnish add parsley and salt.

Cooked Salad
Kochsalat auf Wiener Art

Trim off the ends of the leaves, discarding any that are discoloured. Cut the rib from each one. Rins in water and pat dry.

Salt the water, bring it to the boil and add the salad. Bring the water back to the boil, then reduce the heat. The salad is tender, when the ribs of the leaves can be pressed easily. Drain and refresh by rinsing under cold running water.

Grab a handful of leaves and roll loosely into a bunch. Then cut into strips of the desired width. Heat butter in a sauté pan, add finely chopped onions and sprinkle with some flour. Add parsley, turn and toss and pour in some beef stock. Reduce the liquid and pour it, through a sieve, over the salad. Cook for some minutes and season to taste with salt, pepper and nutmeg.

Ingredients:

800g (1lb 12 oz) cooking salad

40g (1 ½ oz) butter

60g (2 oz) onions

40g (1 ½ oz) flour

fresh parsley finely chopped

beef stock

salt

pepper

nutmeg

Beans with Dill
Dillfisolen

Put the washed and cut green beans in boiling water, then reduce heat and gently simmer the vegetables. Heat butter in a sauté pan, add finely chopped onions and sprinkle with some flour. Add dill, turn and toss and pour in some beef stock. Reduce the liquid and pour it through a sieve over the green beans. Season to taste with salt, pepper, vinegar, sugar and chopped dill.

Add the whisked sour cream, bring it to short boil and let it rest.

Ingredients:

800g (1lb 12 oz) green beans

50g (1 ¾ oz) onions

50g (1 ¾ oz) butter

40g (1 ½ oz) flour

½l (16fl oz) beef stock

salt

pepper

a dash of vinegar

sugar

fresh dill, chopped

¼l (8fl oz) sour cream

The Batter
Backteig

Ingredients:
250ml (8fl oz) wine, beer or milk
250g (9 oz) flour, salt
3tbsp oil
3 egg yolks, 3 egg whites
1tbsp sugar

Whisk liquid and flour and stir in salt, oil and egg yolks. In a separate bowl whisk the egg whites with a balloon whisk to soft peaks. Carefully fold in the dough and leave to rest.

Fried Plums
Schlosserbuben

Ingredients:
Basic batter, with milk or wine (see above)
½l (16fl oz) water
100g (3 ½ oz) sugar
1 cinnamon stick, 5 cloves
lemon juice
24 dried prunes/plums
200g (7 oz) almond paste
baking fat
100g (3 ½ oz) grated chocolate
50g (1 ¾ oz) caster sugar

Pour water into a heavy based pan and add sugar, lemon zest, cloves and cinnamon. Bring it to a boil and add the prunes. Cook until tender, and leave to rest over night.

Take two plumes and a piece of the almond paste, press together, form a ball and dip into the batter, piece by piece. Deep fry them in frying pan until golden brown and crisp. Drain on kitchen paper.

Mix the chocolate with the sugar and spread over a plate. Using a fork, roll the balls in the powder.

Fried Apricots
Wiener Wäschermädeln

Ingredients:
Wine batter (see above)
8 fresh apricots, halved and stoned
1/16l (2fl oz) apricot liqueur
icing sugar
200g (7 oz) almond paste
baking fat
icing sugar, vanilla custard

Sprinkle the apricots with liqueur and coat with icing sugar. Take two apricot halves and a piece of the almond paste, press together, form a ball and dip into the batter, piece by piece. Deep fry them in frying pan until golden brown. Drain on paper.

Dust the fried apricots withicing sugar and serve with vanilla custard.

Photo: Fried Apricots

Potato Dough
Kartoffelteig

Ingredients:

300g (10 ½ oz) floury
potatoes, unpeeled and
cooked
120g (4 oz) flour,
30g (1 oz) fine semolina
salt
30g (1 oz) butter, 2 egg yolks

Peel the warm potatoes, leave to rest for some minutes, then pass through a ricer or food mill. Add the melted butter, flour, semolina and the egg yolks. Combine these ingredients with the potatoes, and carefully fold in the flour. Knead the dough quickly.

Apricot Dumplings
Marillenknödel

Ingredients:

Potato batter (see above)
8 fresh apricots, stoned
8 lump sugar
90g (3 ¼ oz) butter
150g (5 ½ oz) bread crumbs,
roasted in melted butter
icing sugar

Dig out the stones with the shaft of a wooden spoon and replace the stone with a piece of lump sugar. Take the dough, and roll it into the form of a cylinder shape 5cm. Using a sharp knife, cut each cylinder into slices and flatten the dough with your hand or the back of a table spoon. Draw the dough up over each apricot to form a sealed dumpling. Drop the dumplings into boiling water and cook for about 12–15 minutes until they rise to the top. Lift out the dumplings with a slotted spoon and roll them in the bread crumbs. When serving sprinkle with icing sugar.

Plum Dumplings
Zwetschkenknödel

Ingredients:

Potato dough (see above)
8 fresh plums
8 lump sugar
90g (3 ¼ oz) butter
150g (5 ½ oz) bread
crumbs
icing sugar

Dig out the stones with the shaft of a wooden spoon and replace the stone with a piece of lump sugar. Take the dough, and roll it into the form of a cylinder shape 5 cm. Using a sharp knife, cut each cylinder into slices and flatten the dough with your hand or the back of a table spoon. Draw the dough up over each plum to form a sealed dumpling. Drop the dumplings into boiling water and cook for about 12–15 minutes until they rise to the top. Lift out the dumplings with a slotted spoon and roll them in the bread crumbs. When serving sprinkle with icing sugar.

Photo: Plum Dumplings

Pancakes
Palatschinkenteig

Combine all the ingredients in a bowl and whisk with a whisking balloon to make a smooth batter. Cover and leave to rest for 20 minutes. The batter should have the consistence of a single cream, if necessary, add a little more milk.

Heat a pan with a pinch of oil or concentrated butter. Remove from the heat and laddle a small amount of batter into the pan. Swirl the batter around, so that the bottom of the pan is evenly coated. Cook on both sides until brown. Turn it to plate and pile them up, while you cook the remainder.

Pancakes with Apricot Jam
Marillenpalatschinken

Ingredients:

Pancake batter (see above)
300g (10 ½ oz) apricot jam
a dash of rum, icing sugar

Pass the jam through a sieve and season with rum. Spread the jam on the pancakes, roll loosely and sprinkle with icing sugar.

Pancakes with Curd
Topfenpalatschinken

Ingredients:

Pancake batter (see above)
50g (1 ¾ oz) butter
30g (1 oz) icing sugar
vanilla sugar
grated zest of lemon
3 egg yolks, 3 egg whites
125ml (4fl oz) sour cream
250g (9 oz) curd cheese
(10 %), sieved
40g (1 ½ oz) granulated sugar
30g (1 oz) raisins

For the topping:
125ml (4fl oz) milk
1 egg, 1 egg yolk
30g (1 oz) granulated sugar
3tbsp sour cream
icing sugar

Whisk butter with icing sugar, vanille sugar and lemon zest in a bowl until creamy. Stir in egg yolk , sour cream and the sieved curd cheese. Beat the white of the egg stiff and carefully fold it in the curd mixture and add the raisins. Spread the filling evenly on a pancake, roll it loosely and cut in halves. Stand the stuffed pancake halves upright in two rows into a deep baking tin and bake in the preheated oven by 180 °C for 10 minutes. Remove the pan from the oven. For the topping mix all the ingredients and pour it on top of the pancakes. Back in oven and bake for another 15 minutes. Sprinkle with icing sugar.

Strudel Dough
Strudelteig (gezogen)

Ingredients:

250g (9 oz) plain white flour, sifted

2tbsp oil

salt

approx. 125ml (4fl oz) warm water

Place the flour, warm water, oil and salt in a bowl and knead until a dough forms, preferably with an electric mixer. Shape into a ball, brush with oil and leave to rest for ½ hour.

Lay a large cotton cloth on a table and dredge with flour. Put the dough in the centre and sift over a little flour. Pat the dough into a square then roll out into a large rectangle. To stretch the dough, flour your hands and slip them, palms down, under the centre of the dough. Working towards the nearest edge, move your hands apart repeatedly whilst gently stretching and pulling the dough. Move round the table stretching a section of dough at a time until it is thin enough. Cut off the thick borders which will build up around the edges.

Apple Strudel
Apfelstrudel

Ingredients:

Strudel dough (see above)

For the filling:

500g (1lb 2 oz) cox's apples or similar, peeled, sliced

30g (1 oz) bread crumbs

30g (1 oz) butter

30g (1 oz) raisins

40g (1 ½ oz) granulated sugar

1tsp grounded cinnamon

clarified butter to brush

icing sugar to sprinkle

Spread the filling thick in a strip along the edge nearest to you. Brush the pastry edges with clarified butter.

Fold in the side edges of the pastry. Using the cloth to help lift the dough, roll the strudel into a fairly loose roll. Place the strudel seam-side down, onto a large baking tray or into a deep roasting tin. Brush the strudel with cold, clarified butter. Bake for 25 minutes with 200 °C. Brush once more with butter. Remove from the oven, sprinkle with icing sugar and serve warm.

Curd Cheese Strudel

Topfenstrudel

Ingredients:

Strudel dough (see p. 74)

For the filling:

60g (2 oz) butter
30g (1 oz) icing sugar
salt, vanilla sugar,
grated zest of 1 lemon
2 egg yolks
250g (9 oz) curd cheese (10 %), sieved
125ml (4fl oz) soured cream
2 egg whites, beaten stiff thick sugar
30g (1 oz) plain flour, sifted
40g (1 ½ oz) raisins
clarified butter to brush
125ml (4fl oz) milk
icing sugar to garnish

Whisk butter with icing sugar, vanille sugar and lemon zest in a bowl until creamy. Stir in egg yolk , soured cream and the sieved curd cheese. Beat the white of the egg stiff and carefully fold it in the curd mixture and the flour.

Spread the filling thick on 2/3 of the pastry and sprinkle with raisins. Brush the rest with butter.

Fold in the side edges of the pastry. Using the cloth to help lift the dough, roll the strudel into a fairly loose roll. Place the strudel seam-side down, onto a large baking tray or into a deep roasting tin. Brush the strudel with cold, clarified butter. Bake for 20 minutes with 180 °C. Pour hot milk over the strudels and bake for another 20 minutes.

Sprinkle with icing sugar and serve with vanilla custard.

Hot Vanilla Custard

Vanillesauce

Ingredients:

½l (16fl oz) milk
100g (3 ½ oz) granulated sugar
20 g (¾ oz)
vanilla sugar
2 egg yolks
rum

Heat half of the milk with sugar. Mix the rest of the milk with the vanilla sugar and egg yolks and pour it in the boiling milk, whisking constantly with a balloon whisk. Reduce the heat, give a short hard boil and leave to cool. Season with rum to taste.

You can enrich the custard if you replace half of the milk with cream.

Béchamel Omelette

Melt unsalted butter in a pan. Mix together flour, milk and salt and add to the melted butter, whisking until the sauce thickens. Reduce heat and stir in the egg yolks.

Beat the white of the egg with sugar until it is thick and carefully fold it in the béchamel mixture.

Heat butter in a pan and put one quarter of the batter into the pan. Bake at reduced heat on both sides.

Ingredients:

50g (1 ¾ oz) unsalted butter

50g (1 ¾ oz) plain flour

3/8l (13fl oz) milk

salt

4 egg yolks

4 egg whites

30g (1 oz) granulated sugar

butter

Emperors Omelette
Kaiseromelette

Pass the jam through a sieve and season with rum. Spread the jam on the béchamel omelette, fold together and sprinkle with icing sugar.

Ingredients:

Béchamel Omelette (see above)

apricot jam

icing sugar

Baked Yeast Buns
Buchteln

Ingredients:

125ml (4fl oz) milk, warmed or lukewarm

20g (¾ oz) yeast

30g (1 oz) icing sugar

30g (1 oz) butter

a dash of salt

250g (9 oz) strong plain flour

2 egg yolks

vanilla sugar

lemon zest

150g (5 ½ oz) plum jam

1 tbsp rum

cinnamon

butter

icing sugar

For the yeast sponge batter, crumble the fresh yeast, or sprinkle the dried, onto the warm milk in a mixing bowl. Sift in the flour and knead until the mixture is smooth. Cover with a cloth, and leave to rise in a warm place.

To make the main yeast mixture, sift in the flour and salt together, add the milk, egg yolks, sugar, lemon zest, and the vanilla. Knead until it forms a smooth dough. Add then the risen sponge batter and knead with a dough hook, until it has large air bubbles. Put it aside, cover with a cloth and leave to rise for 20 minutes in a cool place.

Roll out the dough to the size 30 x 30 cm (12 x 12 in) and cut in squares of 5 x 5 cm (2 x 2 in). Mix plum jam with rum and cinnamon, place the filling in the middle of the cubes and close the edges tightly at the top. Dip each bun in melted butter and place them closely side-by-side in a well buttered baking tray facing down the folded edges.

Cover with a cloth a leave to rise in a warm place for 20 minutes. Bake in the preheated oven, set the temperature to 180 °C, for about 25 minutes. Leave to cool and dredge with icing sugar.

Esterhazy Slices
Esterhazyschnitten

Ingredients:

7 egg yolks

50g (1 ¾ oz) granulated sugar

vanilla sugar

grated zest of lemon

7 egg whites

130g (4 ½ oz) granulated sugar

230g (8 oz) grounded hazelnuts

oil and flour to batter the baking tray

For the cream:

250g (9 oz) butter

100g (3 ½ oz) icing sugar

250ml (8fl oz) vanilla cream

1tbsp rum

For the vanilla cream:

1/4l (8fl oz) milk

20g (¾ oz) vanilla sugar

40g (1 ½ oz) icing sugar

20g (¾ oz) vanilla custard powder

1 egg yolk

For the garnitur:

40g (1 ½ oz) apricot jam, strained

250g (9 oz) fondant – sugar glaze

1tsp cacao – chocolate powder

50g (1 ¾ oz) grated almonds, roasted

For the cream beat the butter with icing sugar creamy. Pass the vanilla cream through a fine sieve and pour slowly onto the cream butter, add rum and stir continuously.

For the vanilla cream pour ¼ of the milk into a bowl, blend in the egg yolks, the sugar and the vanilla powder. Bring the rest of the milk to a boil and pour in the egg yolk mixture, stir well and remove from the heat immediately.

Beat the egg yolk with 50g granulated sugar, vanilla sugar and lemon zest creamy. Take the egg whites, 130g granulated sugar and whisk together until the mixture is white and thick. Fold into the egg yolk mixture, add the grated hazelnuts and gently mix together. Turn the mixture out onto a baking tray and spread lightly (5 mm). Bake for about 8 minutes, remove from oven and let it cool. Cut in 8 cm stripes. Spread butter cream on bottom layer, cover with the second layer, spread cream again and so forth. Sandwich with the top layer smooth side upwards and spread some reserved cream on the sides of the cake. Let it cool.

Spread over the top layer the strained apricot jam and glaze with the warm fondant. Take 2 tbsp of fondant and mix with the chocolate (cacao). Fill the mixture in a small piping bag and pipe lengthsways in lines. While the fondant is still warm, create the typical esterhazy pattern dragging a knife lengthwise across in thin lines. Leave to set and sprinkle the sides of the cake with the almonds. Cut in 10 slices.

Traditional Doughnuts
Faschingskrapfen

Ingredients:

125ml (4fl oz) full fat milk
20g (¾ oz) yeast
250g (9 oz) plain flour
2 egg yolks
25g (1 oz) caster sugar
40g (1 ½ oz) butter
1tsp rum
a dash of salt
zest of 1 lemon
baking fat for deep frying
icing sugar for dusting
apricot jam, sieved

For the yeast sponge batter, crumble the fresh yeast, or sprinkle the dried, onto the warm milk in mixing bowl. Sift in the flour and knead until the mixture is smooth . Cover with a cloth, and leave to rise in a warm place.

Whisk egg yolk, sieved icing sugar, rum, salt and lemon zest until thick and creamy. Heat the rest of the milk with butter and combine the dough with flour and the risen sponge batter until just combined. With slightly floured hands shape the dough into a ball, cover with cloth, and leave to rest for 20 minutes.

Roll out the dough to pieces of 40g. Form balls and place on a floured cloth. Sprinkle with flour, press the balls in shape with a plate and let it rise again.

In a deep pan heat the oil to 180 °C. Use a draining spoon to gently lay the doughnuts one at a time in the hot oil. Fry on each side until golden brown. Lift out and drain on kitchen paper. Fill with a teaspoon of strained apricot jam and dust the warm doughnuts with icing sugar for serving.

Shredded Pancakes

Kaiserschmarren

Ingredients:

375ml (13fl oz) milk

120g (4 oz) plain flour, sifted

salt

lemon zest

vanilla sugar

4 egg yolks

4 egg whites

50g (1 ¾ oz) granulated sugar

50g (1 ¾ oz) butter

icing sugar

Combine the milk, flour, salt, lemon zest, vanilla sugar and egg yolks in a bowl and whisk until smooth. In a separate bowl whisk the egg whites with granulated sugar until it forms soft peaks. Fold the white gently through the batter.

Heat a large frying pan and pour in batter to a depth of 3 cm. Sprinkle with raisins. Bake on reduced heat, and when the bottom is slightly brown, cut the pancake in halve, turn it around and place the pan in the preheated oven. Bake for 15 minutes at 180 °C. Remove from the oven, and break the pancake in smaller, unregular sized pieces, using two forks. Add some melted butter, toss well and put it back in the oven for a short while.

When serving dust with icing sugar.

Plum Compote

Zwetschkenröster

Ingredients:

1kg (2lb 4oz) plums, halved and stoned

125ml (4fl oz) water

200g (7 oz) granulated sugar

cinnamon sticks

cloves

Heat water with sugar, cinnamon and cloves. Bring it to a boil and add the plums. Reduce the heat and cook it slowly to a stew.

Let it cool and remove the spices.

Noodles with Poppy Seeds
Mohnnudeln

Ingredients:

Potato dough (p. 70)
80g (2 ¾ oz) grounded poppy seeds
50g (1 ¾ oz) butter
icing sugar

Roll the dough with your hands into a long thin sausage shape on a lightly flour-dusted surface. Divide into smaller pieces and roll with your fingertips until very thin. Place the noodles in large pot with plenty of fast-boiling, salted water, reduce heat, and simmer covered for about 5 minutes.

In a frying pan heat butter, add the drained noodles, the poppy seeds and sugar. Toss well, make sure all noodles are coated. Serve immediately.

Hazelnut Ring Cake
Nusskranzkuchen

Ingredients:

200g (7 oz) butter
200g (7 oz) icing sugar
200g (7 oz) flour
4 egg yolks
4 egg whites
100g (3 ½ oz) hazelnuts, chopped
100g (3 ½ oz) chocolate, curls oder rasped
1 dash of grounded cinnamon
1tsp vanilla sugar
2tsp baking powder
2 apples, peeled, shredded
butter and flour for the mould
icing sugar for dusting

Combine butter, vanilla sugar and half of the granulated sugar, mix in the egg yolks in portions and beat until thick and creamy. Whisk the egg whites with sugar until it forms soft peaks. Mix apples, hazelnuts and the chocolate. Combine the flour with baking powder and cinnamon. Carefully fold in the yolk mixture, the stiff egg white, the flour and the apples mixture.

Prepare a ring mould by brushing with melted butter and dust with and fill in the mixture. Place the cake in the preheated oven and bake at a temperature of 170 °C for about 60 minutes.

Remove from the oven and leave until cool, before turning onto a wire rack. Dust with icing sugar to serve.

Photo: Hazelnut ring cake

Marble Gugelhupf

Marmorgugelhupf

Ingredients:

80g (2 ¾ oz) butter

70g (2 ½ oz) oil

100g (3 ½ oz) icing sugar

lemon zest

vanilla sugar

4 egg yolks

60g (2 oz) plain white flour, sifted

1tsp baking powder, sifted

125ml (4fl oz) milk

4 egg whites

100g (3 ½ oz) granulated sugar

200g (7 oz) flour

60g (2 oz) chocolate

butter and flour for the mould

icing sugar

Prepare a gugelhupf mould by brushing with melted butter and dust with .

For the batter beat butter, oil, icing sugar, lemon zest, vanilla sugar and egg yolks until thick and creamy. Mix in portions of baking powder then milk, beating well between additions. Spoon in 1/2 of the mixture the melted chocolate and whisk together until smooth.

Whisk the egg whites with sugar until it forms soft peaks and fold it as well as the flour halvewise in both mixtures. For the marble effect, spread a layer of pale mixture in the mould, then place alternate the dark batter.

Place in the preheated oven and bake at a temperature of 170 °C for about 60 minutes.

Turn the cake out onto a wire rack to cool. Dust with icing sugar to serve.

Chocolate Hazelnut Pudding
Mohr im Hemd

Cut the bread in small cubes and soak with milk. Then press out the liquid and strain the bread through a sieve.

Combine butter with sifted icing sugar and beat until creamy. Stir in portionwise the egg yolks, bread paste and the melted chocolate. Whisk the egg whites with icing sugar until the forms soft peaks and fold into the mixture. Mix the walnuts with bread crumbs, and add that to the mixture as well.

Prepare pudding moulds by brushing with melted butter and dust with icing and set the moulds on a deep baking tray.

Fill the mixture in a large piping bag and fill the moulds with the mixture. Pour boiling water up the depths of 2 cm on the baking tray and bake in the preheated oven at 170 °C for about 40 minutes.

 When finished turn the cakes out, pour chocolate sauce on top and garnish with whipped cream.

Ingredients:

1 ½ bread roll, remove the rind, cut in cubes
125ml (4fl oz) milk
80g (2 ¾ oz) butter
30g (1 oz) icing sugar
60g (2 oz) chocolate
4 egg yolks
4 egg whites
60g (2 oz) granulated sugar
50g (1 ¾ oz) walnuts, grated
30g (1 oz) bread crumbs
butter
icing sugar
chocolate sauce
250ml (8fl oz) sweet cream

Carinthian Cake

Kärntner Reindling

Ingredients:

For the yeast sponge batter:

500g (1lb 2 oz) strong plain flour

20g (¾ oz) yeast

100g (3 ½ oz) butter

250ml (8fl oz) lukewarm milk

1 egg

1 egg yolk

50g (1 ¾ oz) granulated sugar

salt

aniseed

gingerbread spices

For the filling:

80g (2 ¾ oz) butter

100g (3 ½ oz) granulated sugar

2tbsp cinnamon, powder

100g (3 ½ oz) raisins

For the yeast sponge batter, mix the siftet flour with sugar, crumble the fresh yeast or sprinkle the dried, onto warm milk in a mixing bowl and leave to rise, covered, for 10 minutes.

To make the main yeast mixture, add the rest of the ingredients and knead until it forms a smooth dough. Put it aside, cover with a cloth and leave to rise in a warm place.

Before rolling out, knead the dough once more. Then roll out the dough on a lightly floured surface until 1 cm thick. Spread the filling mixture over the dough and roll up with gentle pressure.

Lay the roll in a buttered baking tray in form of snail-shell or use a Gugelhupf or a Ringcake mould.

Bake in the preheated oven at 180 °C for about 60 minutes and turn the cake out of the form. As a variation add to the filling apples.

Sachertorte

Ingredients:

180g (6 oz) butter

80g (2 ¾ oz) icing sugar

1tsp vanilla sugar

8 egg yolks

180g (6 oz) best quality
dark chocolate

8 egg whites

150g (5 ½ oz) granulated
sugar

180g (6 oz) plain white
flour

180g (6 oz) apricote jam,
boiled and strained

For the chocolate glaze:

400g (14 oz) sugar

330g (12 oz) best quality
dark cooking chocolate

250ml (8fl oz) water

Grease the sides of a springform cake tin and dust with flour.

Whisk the butter with sugar and vanilla seeds until pale. Add the egg yolks, a little at the time, beating well between each addition. Gently pour in the melted chocolate. Whisk together the egg whites and the sugar. Beat until thick and creamy. Carefully fold the egg whites and the flour and pour in the prepared springform tin.

Bake in a preheated oven for about 60 minutes at 170 °C.

For the glace mix all the ingredients together and bring to a boil. Stir gently with a balloon whisk and cook on low heat for 5 minutes. Steadily whisk, as the mixture cools.

Slightly dust with flour and remove the cake from the oven and turn over onto a wire rack or a paper sheet. Slice the cake through the middle. Spread with apricot jam. Carefully replace the top layer.

Make the chocolate glaze and pour straight onto the apricot-glazed surface of the cake. Using a palette knife spread out the glaze.

Cut in slices and serve with whipped cream.

Salzburger Nockerln

Ingredients:

5 egg whites
40g (1 ½ oz) granulated
sugar
1tsp icing sugar
3 egg yolks
20g (¾ oz) plain flour
lemon zest
a dash of vanilla sugar
65ml (2fl oz) milk
40g (1 ½ oz) butter
icing sugar and vanilla
sugar to dust

Combine butter, icing sugar, milk and vanilla sugar and heat it up in a deep roasting tin or a baking tray.

Whisk 4 egg whites with granulated sugar until thick and creamy. Quickly fold in the egg yolks, flour and lemon zest.

Form 3 large sized nockerl, place them in the pan and bake for 7 minutes with 180 °C until golden brown.

Dust with the sugar-mix and serve immediately.